DATE DUE

AUG 0 8 2014	
DEC 0 7 2014	

BRODART, CO.   Cat. No. 23-221

Pterodactyl

Aaron Carr

LET'S READ
AV2
BY WEIGL™
ADDED VALUE • AUDIO VISUAL

www.av2books.com

LET'S READ
AV²
BY WEIGL™
ADDED VALUE · AUDIO VISUAL

Go to **www.av2books.com**, and enter this book's unique code.

BOOK CODE

C130739

AV² by Weigl brings you media enhanced books that support active learning.

AV² provides enriched content that supplements and complements this book. Weigl's AV² books strive to create inspired learning and engage young minds in a total learning experience.

Your AV² Media Enhanced books come alive with...

 Audio
Listen to sections of the book read aloud.

 Video
Watch informative video clips.

 Embedded Weblinks
Gain additional information for research.

 Try This!
Complete activities and hands-on experiments.

 Key Words
Study vocabulary, and complete a matching word activity.

 Quizzes
Test your knowledge.

 Slide Show
View images and captions, and prepare a presentation.

... and much, much more!

Published by AV² by Weigl
350 5th Avenue, 59th Floor New York, NY 10118
Website: www.av2books.com   www.weigl.com

Library of Congress Control Number: 2013937448
ISBN 978-1-62127-239-7 (hardcover)
ISBN 978-1-62127-245-8 (softcover)

Printed in the United States of America in North Mankato, Minnesota
1 2 3 4 5 6 7 8 9 0 17 16 15 14 13

052013
WEP040413

Project Coordinator: Aaron Carr   Art Director: Terry Paulhus

All illustrations by Jon Hughes, pixel-shack.com; Getty Images: 19 inset; Alamy: 20.

Pterodactyl

In this book,
you will learn

what its
name means

what it
looked like

where it lived

what it ate

and much more!

Meet the pterodactyl. Its name means "winged fingers."

Pterodactyl was not a dinosaur.
It was a flying reptile
called a pterosaur.

Pterodactyl had wings
up to three feet wide.
It had one long finger
that it used to flap its wings.

9

Pterodactyl was a meat eater.
It ate fish and other small animals.

Pterodactyl had a very long jaw
with almost 100 sharp teeth.
It had a small hooked beak
at the end of each jaw.

13

Pterodactyl walked slowly when it was on the ground. It walked on its hands and feet.

Pterodactyl lived in trees
and caves near water.

It could be found
in parts of Europe and Africa.

Pterodactyls died out
about 150 million years ago.

People learned about them from fossils.

20

People can go to museums to see fossils and learn more about pterodactyls.

Pterodactyl Facts

These pages provide detailed information that expands on the interesting facts found in the book. They are intended to be used by adults as a learning support to help young readers round out their knowledge of each amazing dinosaur or pterosaur featured in the *Discovering Dinosaurs* series.

Pages 4–5

Pterodactyl means "winged finger." Though pterodactyl is a better-known name, this prehistoric animal's real name is Pterodactylus. The Pterodactylus was named for its long fourth fingers, which provided support for most of each wing. There were many different species of Pterodactylus. They ranged in size from as small as a sparrow to about the size of an albatross, one of the largest birds in the world today.

Pages 6–7

Pterodactylus was not a dinosaur. Dinosaurs were prehistoric reptiles that walked on land, while the Pterodactylus was a prehistoric reptile that could fly. For this reason, the Pterodactylus is not considered a dinosaur. Instead, it is part of a group of flying reptiles called pterosaurs. Pterosaurs lived in all parts of the world at the same time as the dinosaurs. Pterosaurs ranged in size from the small Pterodactylus to the massive Quetzalcoatlus, which stood as tall as a giraffe and had a 40-foot (12-meter) wingspan.

Pages 8–9

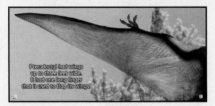

Pterodactylus had wings up to 3 feet (1 meter) wide. The Pterodactylus had long, thin wings covered in skin. It had three fingers sticking out of the top middle part of the wing. The fourth finger on each wing extended about half the total length of the wing. The wing was formed by skin and muscle that stretched from the arm and long finger to the hind legs.

Pages 10–11

Pterodactylus was a carnivore, or meat-eater. The Pterodactylus was a carnivore that primarily ate fish and small animals. It is believed the Pterodactylus flew over bodies of water and swooped down to catch fish swimming near the surface. Scientists believe the diet of Pterodactylus may have included crabs, mollusks, and insects.

Pterodactylus had a very long jaw with almost 100 sharp teeth. The Pterodactylus's narrow jaw made up about three-quarters of the total length of its skull. Unlike other pterosaurs, which had jaws that curved upward, the Pterodactylus had a straight jaw. When young, its teeth were wide and cone-shaped. As it grew older, its teeth became narrower and more numerous.

Pterodactylus walked slowly on its wings and feet. The Pterodactylus walked on all fours, using both its hind legs and its front claws. The rest of the wing folded and pointed up while the Pterodactylus walked. This is very similar to how modern-day bats walk. Scientists do not believe Pterodactylus was very fast when flying, but they think it was able to fly long distances.

Pterodactylus lived in Europe and Africa. The Pterodactylus is believed to have lived mostly in what is now Germany. Scientists believe the Pterodactylus lived in trees or caves near large bodies of water. They did this to stay close to their primary source of food. Living in caves and trees would have also offered some protection against predatory dinosaurs.

Pterodactylus lived about 150 million years ago during the Late Jurassic Period. All that people have learned about the Pterodactylus has come from studying fossils. Fossils form when an animal dies and is covered in sand, mud, or water. This keeps the hard parts of the body, such as bones, teeth, and claws, from decomposing. The body is pressed between layers of mud and sand. Over millions of years, the layers turn into stone, and the animal's bones and teeth turn into stone as well. This preserves the size and shape of the animal.

People can go to museums to see fossils and learn more about the Pterodactylus. Every year, people from all around the world visit museums to see Pterodactylus fossils. More than 20 Pterodactylus fossils have been found, and most of them are complete skeletons. These fossils are often part of permanent exhibits in large museums. Sometimes, they travel to small museums for short exhibits. The American Museum of Natural History in New York has many pterosaur fossils on display, including Pterodactylus.

KEY WORDS

Research has shown that as much as 65 percent of all written material published in English is made up of 300 words. These 300 words cannot be taught using pictures or learned by sounding them out. They must be recognized by sight. This book contains 53 common sight words to help young readers improve their reading fluency and comprehension. This book also teaches young readers several important content words, such as proper nouns. These words are paired with pictures to aid in learning and improve understanding.

Page	Sight Words First Appearance
4	its, means, name, the
7	a, it, not, was
8	feet, had, long, one, that, three, to, up, used
11	and, animals, other, small
12	almost, at, each, end, long, of, very, with
15	hands, on, walked, when
16	in, lived, near, trees, water
17	be, could, found, parts
18	about, out, years
19	from, people, them
21	can, go, learn, more, see

Page	Content Words First Appearance
4	fingers, pterodactyl (pronounced: ter-uh-DAK-til)
7	dinosaur, pterosaur, reptile
8	wings
11	fish, meat eater
12	beak, jaw, teeth
15	ground
16	caves
17	Africa, Europe
19	fossils
21	museums